WHAT MAYA ANGELOU SAYS

THE OFFICIAL COLLECTION

WHAT

MAYA
ANGELOU

SAYS

Quadrille

One of the most significant voices of her generation, Dr Maya Angelou was a writer, poet, civil rights activist and library advocate. The author of numerous works, including *And Still I Rise* (1978) and *I Know Why the Caged Bird Sings* (1969), she is widely recognised as a trailblazer and often graces lists of the most influential Americans.

Born in St. Louis, Missouri in 1928, Angelou's extensive career began as a singer, dancer and composer, before moving to New York in 1960 to begin her writing career in earnest. Over the next decade, her profile as both a writer and a civil rights activist grew, campaigning alongside Malcolm X and Dr. Martin Luther King Jr.

Angelou also garnered a reputation as a compelling spokesperson, lecturing for many years at Wake Forest University and reciting 'On the Pulse of Morning' at the inauguration of Bill Clinton, who would later award her the National Medal of the Arts. This was followed by the Presidential Medal of Freedom under Barack Obama and by the time of her death in 2014, she held over 50 honorary degrees. At her memorial service, Oprah Winfrey and Michelle Obama spoke of her warmth, commitment to equality and education, and the 'affirming power of her words'.

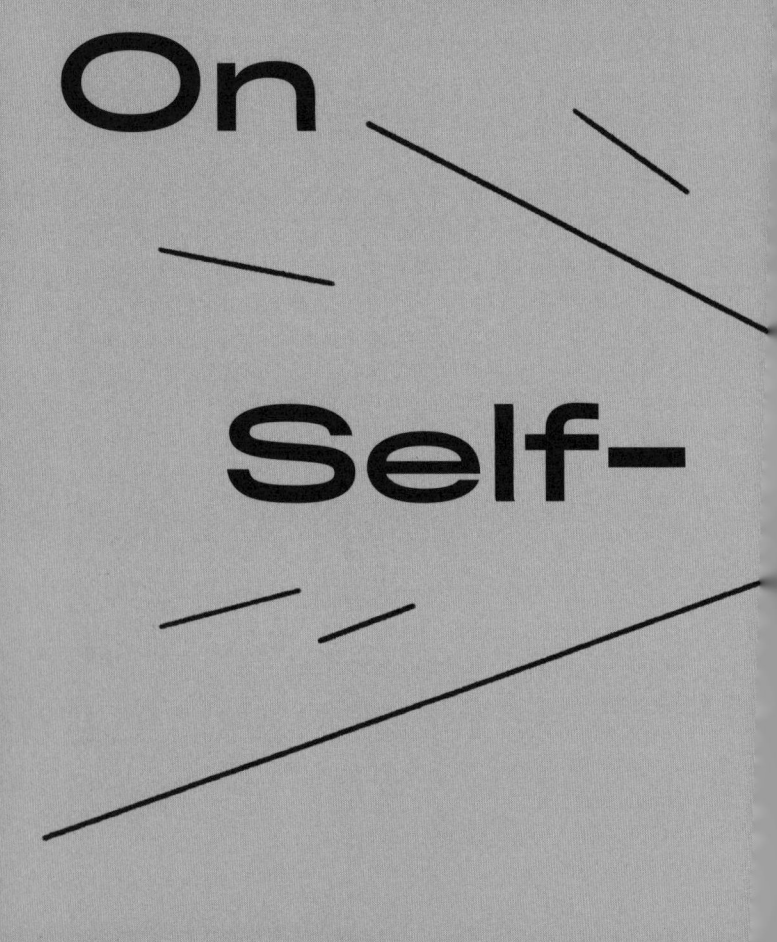

On

Self-

"If you don't like something, change it. If you can't change it, change your attitude."

"We may encounter many defeats, but we must not be defeated."

"I've learned that people will forget what you said, people will forget what you did, but people will never forget how you made them feel." ♡

"It's one of the greatest gifts you can give yourself, to forgive. Forgive everybody."

"The thing to do, it
seems to me, is to
prepare yourself so you
can be a rainbow in
somebody else's cloud.
Somebody who may
not look like you. May
not call God the same
name you call God –
if they call God at all...

I may not dance your dances or speak your language. But be a blessing to somebody. That's what I think."

"I believe that the most <u>important</u> single thing, beyond discipline and <u>creativity</u>, is daring to dare."

"Nothing will work unless you do."

"When you learn, teach. When you get, give."

"You may not
control all the
events that
happen to you,
but you can
decide not to
be reduced
by them."

"If you're always trying to be <u>normal</u>, you will never know how (amazing) you can be."

"Do the best you can
until you know better.
Then when you
know better, do better."

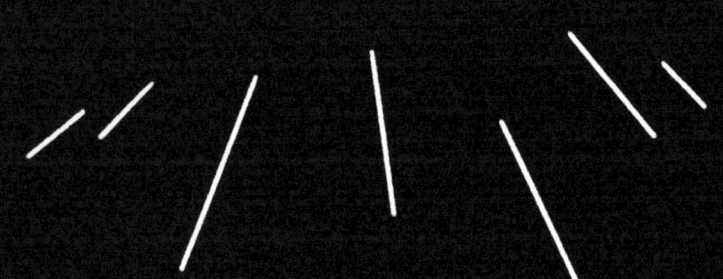

"Nothing can dim the light which shines from within."

"My wish for you is that
you continue. Continue to
be who and how you are,
to astonish a mean world
with your acts of kindness.
Continue to allow humor
to lighten the burden
of your tender heart."

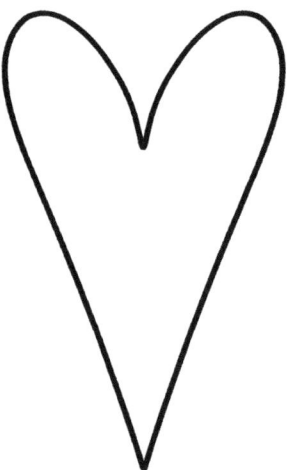

"Develop enough courage
so that you can stand up
for yourself and then stand
up for somebody else."

"It is important that we learn humility, which says there was someone else before me who paid for me."

"One isn't necessarily born with courage, but one is born with potential. Without courage, we cannot practice any other virtue with consistency. We can't be kind, true, merciful, generous, or honest."

On

Love

"Love recognizes no barriers. It jumps hurdles, leaps fences, penetrates walls to arrive at its destination full of hope."

"Whatever you
want to do,
if you want to be
great at it,
you have to love it
and be able to make
sacrifices for it."

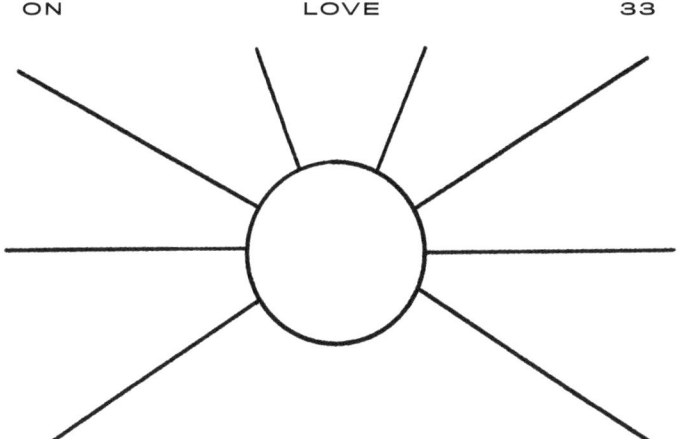

"In the flush of love's
light, we dare be brave
and suddenly we see that
love cost all we are and
will ever be. Yet it is only
love which sets us free."

"If we lose love and self-respect for each other, this is how we finally die."

"Everything of value takes work, particularly relationships."

"The most called-upon prerequisite of a friend is an accessible ear."

"There is an intimate laughter to be found only among friends."

"Yet if we are bold, love strikes away the chains of fear from our souls."

"You can never be great at anything unless you love it."

"Let the brain go to work,
let it meet the heart,
and you will be
able to forgive."

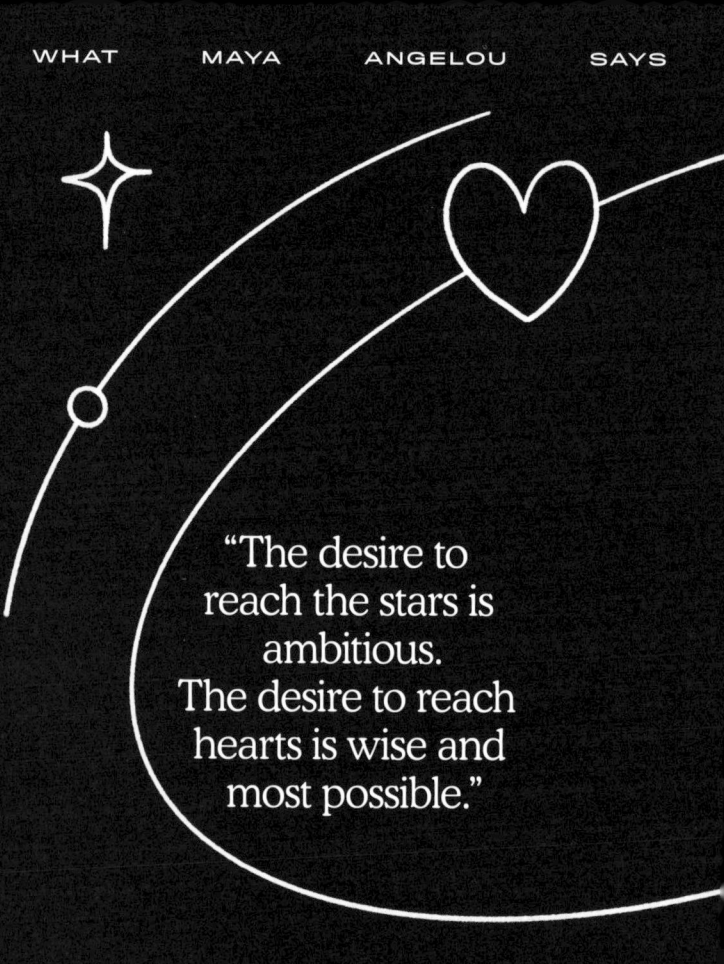

"The desire to reach the stars is ambitious. The desire to reach hearts is wise and most possible."

"We are stronger, kinder, and more generous because we live in an atmosphere where love exists."

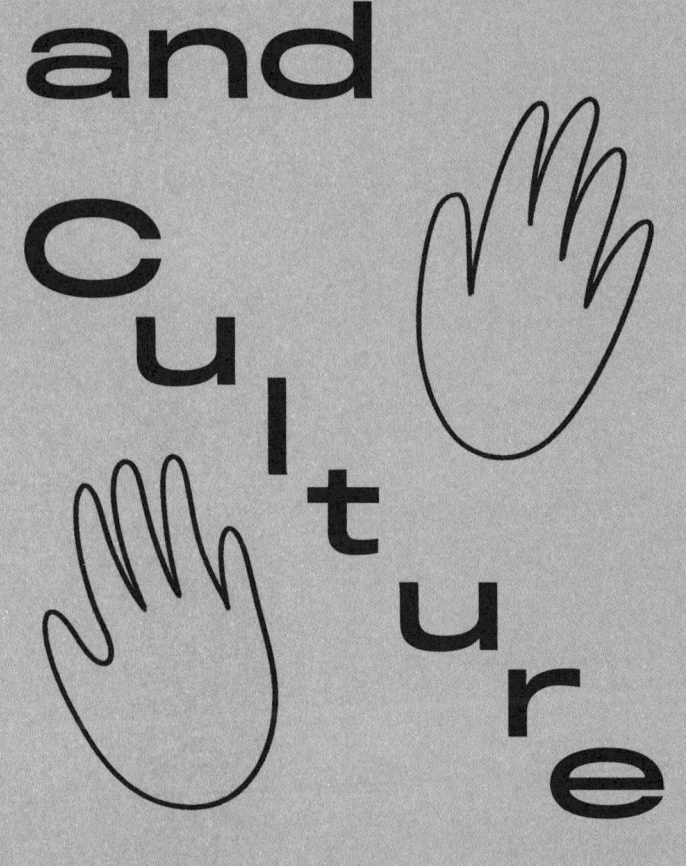

"A Black person grows up in this country – and in many places – knowing that racism will be as familiar as salt to the tongue. And that also, it can be as dangerous as too much salt. I think that you agree that you must struggle for betterment for yourself and for everyone."

"Prejudice is a burden that confuses the past, threatens the future and renders the present inaccessible."

"Hate, it has caused a lot of problems in the world, but has not solved one yet."

"The truth is, no one of us can be free until (everybody) is free."

"We are not our
brother's keeper;
we are our brother
and we are our sister.
We must look past
complexion and
see community."

"How important it is for us to recognize and celebrate our heroes and she-roes!"

"I think a hero is any person really intent on making this a better place for all people."

"We must (wage) ceaseless battle against the forces of greed and hatred...

which
are the
<u>foundations</u>
of all political
inequality."

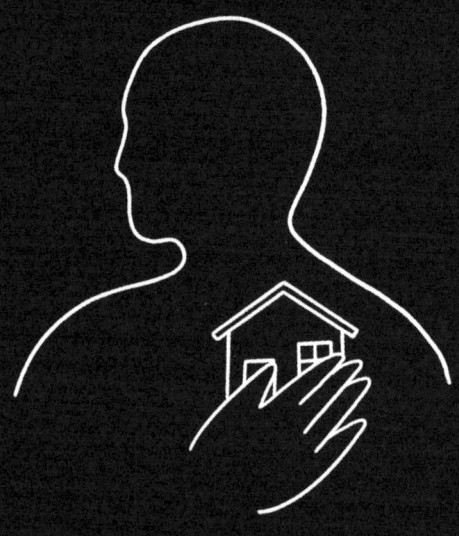

"The ache for home lives
in all of us, the safe place
where we can go as we are
and not be questioned."

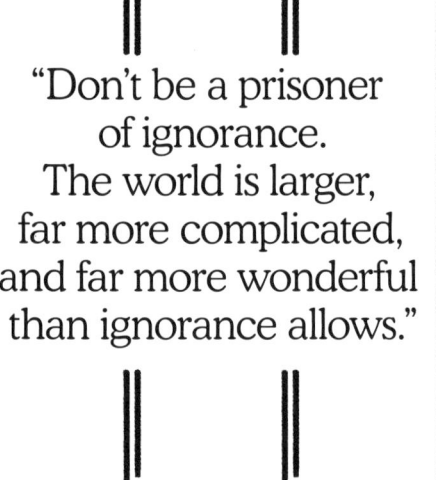

"Don't be a prisoner
of ignorance.
The world is larger,
far more complicated,
and far more wonderful
than ignorance allows."

"Elimination of illiteracy is as serious an issue to our history as the abolition of slavery."

"I believe that each of us
comes from the Creator
trailing wisps of glory."

"I have found that, among its other benefits, giving liberates the soul of the giver."

"When we unite in purpose, we are greater than the sum of our parts."

"Bitterness is like cancer.
It eats upon the host.
But anger is like fire.
It burns it all clean."

"Life loves
to be taken
by the lapel
and told:
'I'm with you,
kid. Let's go.'"

"If one is lucky, a solitary fantasy can totally transform one million realities."

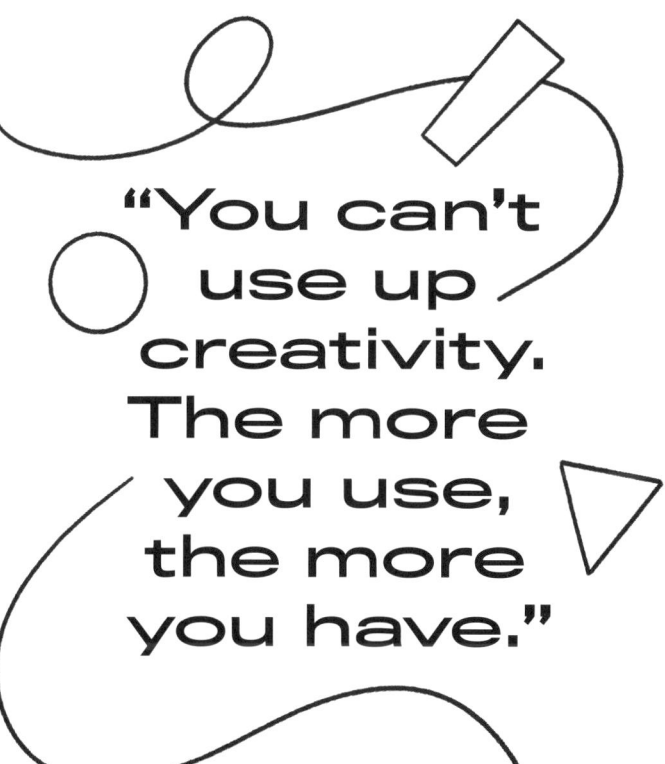

"You can't use up creativity. The more you use, the more you have."

"We delight in the beauty of the butterfly, but rarely admit the changes it has gone through to achieve that beauty."

"When someone shows you who they are, believe them the first time."

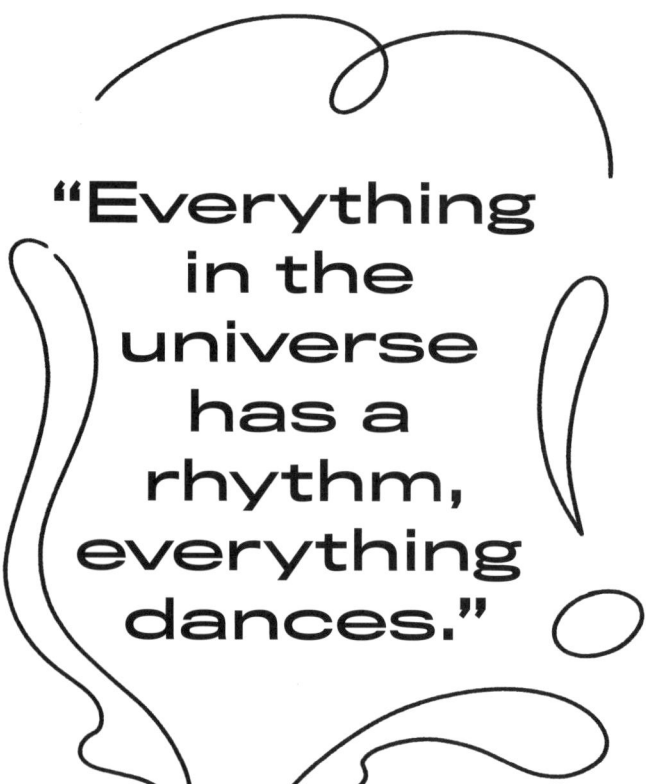

"Everything in the universe has a rhythm, everything dances."

"Do not just teach because that's all you can do. <u>Teach</u> because it's your calling."

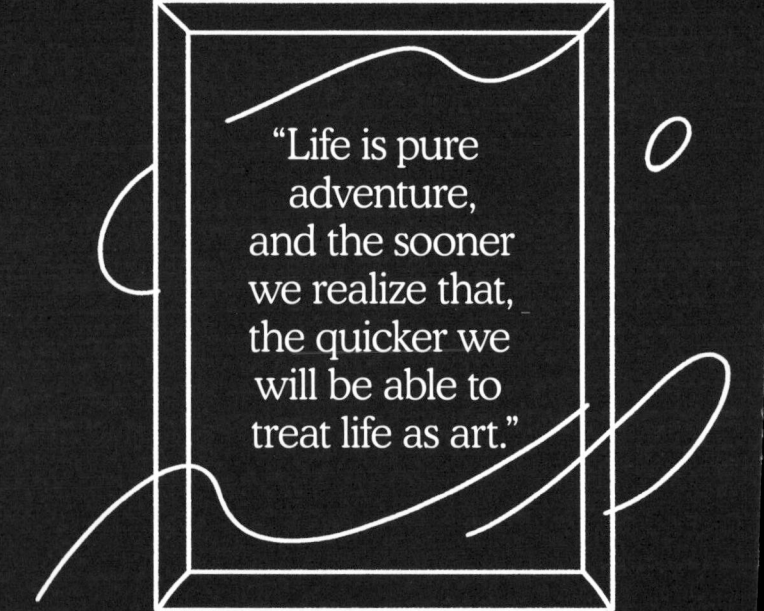

"Life is pure adventure, and the sooner we realize that, the quicker we will be able to treat life as art."

"Laughter and smiles are essential factors in a joyous life."

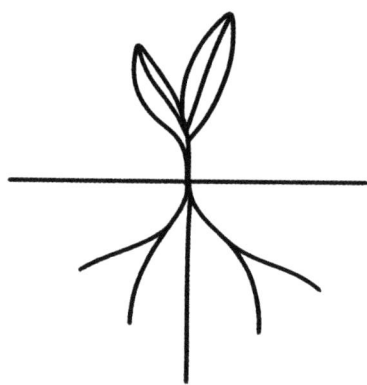

"Those who would use
ridicule as a form of humor,
sow nothing but shame
and bitterness and when
the snide laughter ends,
they will reap only
anger and hostility."

"The idea of overcoming
is always fascinating to me.
It's fascinating because few of
us realize how much <u>energy</u>
we have <u>expended</u> just
to be here today.
I don't think we give
ourselves enough credit
for the overcoming."

"One must nurture the joy in one's life so that it reaches full bloom."

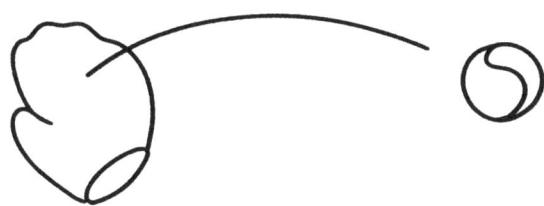

"I've learned that you
shouldn't go through
life with a catcher's
mitt on both hands;
you need to be able to
throw something back."

On

Herself

"I've <u>learned</u> that I still have (a lot) to learn."

"Each time a woman
stands up for herself,
without knowing
it possibly, without
claiming it, she stands
up for all women."

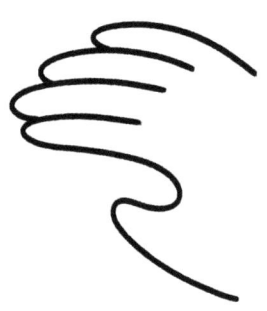

"I refuse to allow any
man-made differences
to separate me from any
other human beings."

"Talent is like electricity. We don't understand electricity. We use it."

"I long, as does every human being, to be at home wherever I find myself."

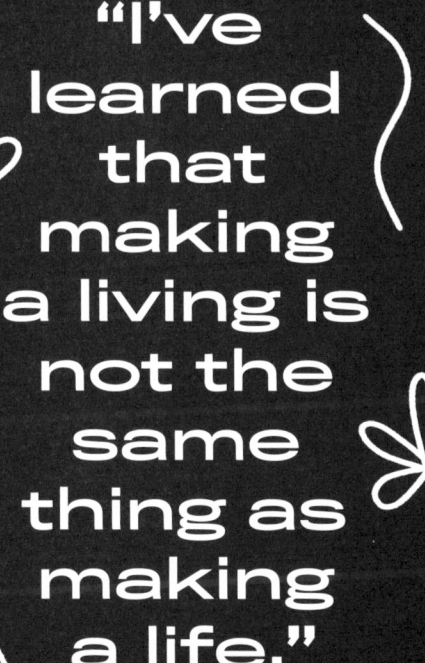

"I've learned that making a living is not the same thing as making a life."

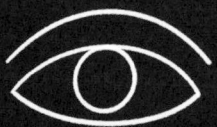

"You are the sum total of everything you've ever seen, heard, eaten, smelled, been told, forgot – it's all there. Everything influences each of us, and because of that, I try to make sure that my experiences are positive."

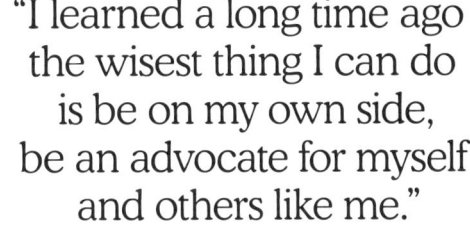

"I learned a long time ago
the wisest thing I can do
is be on my own side,
be an advocate for myself
and others like me."

"Let me tell so much truth. I want to tell the truth in my work. The truth will lead me to the light."

"I always felt, in any town,
if I can get to a library,
I'll be OK.
It really helped me as a child,
and that never left me.
So, I have a special place
for every library,
in my heart of hearts."

"I've learned that whenever I decide something with an open heart, I usually make the right decision."

"My mission in life is not
merely to survive,
but to thrive;
and to do so with
some passion,
some compassion,
some humor,
and some style."

Quadrille, Penguin Random House UK, One Embassy Gardens, 8 Viaduct Gardens, London SW11 7BW

Quadrille Publishing Limited is part of the Penguin Random House group of companies whose addresses can be found at global.penguinrandomhouse.com

Published by Quadrille in 2025

www.penguin.co.uk

A CIP catalogue record for this book is available from the British Library

ISBN 9781784887544

10 9 8 7 6 5 4 3 2 1

Publishing Director: Kajal Mistry
Senior Commissioning Editor: Kate Burkett
Editorial Assistant: Harriet Thornley
Design and Illustration: Double Slice Studio (Amelia Leuzzi and Bonnie Eichelberger)
Production Manager: Sabeena Atchia

Colour reproduction by p2d

Printed in China by RR Donnelley Asia Printing Solution Limited

The authorised representative in the EEA is Penguin Random House Ireland, Morrison Chambers, 32 Nassau Street, Dublin D02 YH68.

MIX
Paper | Supporting responsible forestry
FSC
www.fsc.org
FSC® C018179

Penguin Random House is committed to a sustainable future for our business, our readers and our planet. This book is made from Forest Stewardship Council® certified paper.